CHIEF LITTLE RED CHEEKS

Written by
Emily Lane Waszak

Illustrated by
Sharon Merchant

Published by:

Measure of
Success
PRODUCTIONS

MeasureofSuccess@aol.com

This is dedicated to my loving husband, Jeremy, and our own little chiefs, Robert, Luke, Cassidy, Ainsley, and Levi.

May your lives be filled with adventure and love.

And I also dedicate this to the memory of my mentor and "Pal," Hugh Fox. His inspiration and encouragement will never be forgotten. Abrazos, my friend.

Way up north in the backwoods of Michigan, an old
bear named Annie wanders, eating berries and suet,
just scaring the local folk, the way wild animals
sometimes do. No one's ever seen her up close, at least
no one who ever lived to talk about it, that is.

Well, one day, not too far from Annie's den, a little boy played at his granddad's cabin at the end of the bumpy dirt road.

He went by Chief Little Red Cheeks. He came by that name for a couple of reasons. When looking for adventure, as he often did, he liked to wear an old Indian costume he found in his granddad's basement. And his cheeks burned bright red, radiating the energy he had every time he played hard.

And hard he played, that's for sure.
So his momma began to call him
"Chief Little Red Cheeks."

As Chief Little Red Cheeks started down the wooded
trail, he sang a little song that he made up along the way
about the sun and the trees and the birds in the sky.
The trail wound through stately pines, fields of ferns,
and a lot of dirt and rocks.

Chief Little Red Cheeks picked up a couple of rocks and a feather as he walked and stuffed them into his pocket. "Treasures," he called them, and you just never know when you're going to need treasures.

Suddenly, Chief Little Red Cheeks found himself sloshing through a swamp. Schloop, schloop, the muck sucked at his ankles, and before he knew it, he was knee-deep in the black, tarry pool. Glancing down to assess the situation, he knew his momma was going to be furious about this.

He amazingly made it through without losing his shoes
in the muck of the swamp, but he was coated with it
right up to his knees. Chief Little Red Cheeks did his
figuring, and he figured that the best way out of this
mess was to head to the river and wash off.

To get to that river, though, Chief Little Red Cheeks
had to pass Old Man Benson's place. Old Man
Benson was a gruff old man who didn't take too
kindly to trespassers. The townsfolk swapped stories
about him sitting on his front porch in a rusty seat,
gun in his lap, waiting to shoot at anyone or
anything coming too close to his place.
He didn't like kids, either.
Chief Little Red Cheeks had never seen him, but he
was sure that the old man had to be at least as awful
as those stories said he was. He knew Old Man
Benson was always there, watching and waiting
for his next victim.

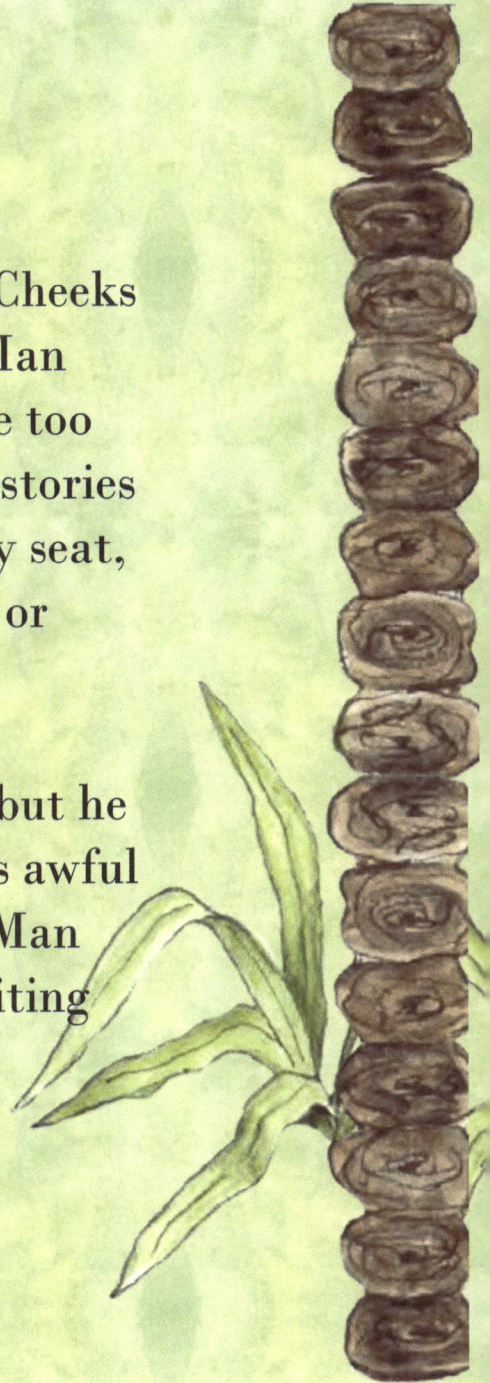

Chief Little Red Cheeks grew closer and closer to Old Man Benson's place. When the tattered cabin was in his sight, he drew a deep breath.

He couldn't quite see the front porch, so he mustered up every ounce of energy and sprinted past the cabin. No sign of Old Man Benson. Relieved, he continued running and began his descent down a pretty steep hill that led to the river.

Suddenly he felt something grasp his ankle and he
fell, dangling on the side of the hill screaming,
"Let me go!"

He heard a snap, and he was loose, tumbling
down that hill like a tumbleweed.
"I ripped that old man's arm right off," he thought as
he kept on rolling, just a big ball of dust spinning down
that hill with chunks of swamp mud from his shoes
flying into the air.
Bumbly tumbly lickity split!

When he finally came to a rest at the bottom of the hill
next to the river, the dust settled and he saw the guilty
grabber, a vine tangled across his shoe.

Weeds stuck out from his tousled hair, grass stains were on his pants, and his face had a big scratch from a stick that poked him real good. He was a mess, but he was safe. Old Man Benson was nowhere in sight.

"Whew!" Chief Little Red Cheeks let out a sigh, and he waded into the water. He watched the mud dissolve from his shoes and swirl with the current of the river. He splashed the fresh, cool water on his face.

Chief Little Red Cheeks glanced into the clear stream to see the dirt fading from his face, but there was still a little bit left. He splashed again and opened his eyes, but as he looked down, he saw two faces staring back.

There, over his shoulder, was Annie, the old backwoods bear with teeth at least a foot long. Now ol' Annie stood at least ten feet tall, Chief Little Red Cheeks was sure, but he was still able to give her a good swat on the nose, just like his granddaddy told him to if ever confronted by a bear, and he took off running.

Chief Little Red Cheeks ran up that hill faster than he
had tumbled down. He knew he had to be running
faster than any man had ever run, but he could still
hear that old bear gaining ground behind him.

Chief Little Red Cheeks had forgotten all about Old Man Benson until he heard a gunshot. He let out a yelp. The blast kept ringing in his ears and he couldn't tell if that old bear was still chasing him or not. He rounded the cabin, and just as he thought he was in the clear, he felt a falcon-like clutch on his shoulder.

The hand lifted him right off of the ground,
and his body went stiff. He slowly turned his neck to see
Old Man Benson, the man no human had ever seen that
closely. The two were nose to crooked nose,
eye to beady eye.
He had a long white beard that barely moved
as the gruff voiced bellowed,
"You all right, boy?"

Chief Little Red Cheeks shakily replied, "Y-y-y-yesss, S-s-s-sir," and he wiggled away and sprinted up the trail, howling the entire way.

His momma heard his screams and ran out of the cabin. "What in the world happened to you?" she exclaimed.

There stood Chief Little Red Cheeks, a muddy mess of river water mixed with dirt resulting in a sludge that dripped from his face, shoes, and pants. He had a scratch across his bright red cheek, and twigs and weeds were still poking through his hair.

"You look like you just tangled with a bear!" she exclaimed, laughing.

If she only knew!

Emily Lane Waszak began writing as a child, and she continues to share this passion as a college instructor. When she is not writing or teaching, she is volunteering in the local schools. Her first book, "Grief: Difficult Times, Simple Steps", was inspired by her volunteer work at a grief center for children. She is currently active in writing instructional texts for educators, including her latest releases with Erik Bean, "Word Press for Student Writing Projects" (Brigantine Media) and "Social Media Writing Lesson Plans" (Westphalia Press), and her children's book "Duck Eggs" (Measure of Success Productions). She resides in Michigan with her husband, Jeremy, and their five children.

www.ingramcontent.com/pod-product-compliance
Lightning Source LLC
Chambersburg PA
CBHW060835270326

41933CB00002B/91